40 Beer Recipes for Home

By: Kelly Johnson

Table of Contents

- Classic Lager
- Pale Ale
- India Pale Ale (IPA)
- Stout
- Porter
- Belgian Witbier
- Hefeweizen
- Pilsner
- Brown Ale
- Scottish Ale
- American Amber Ale
- Irish Red Ale
- Kölsch
- Belgian Dubbel
- Tripel
- Baltic Porter
- American Wheat Beer
- Cream Ale
- Barleywine
- English Bitter
- Berliner Weisse
- Pumpkin Ale
- Fruit-infused Blonde Ale
- Honey Ale
- Coffee Stout
- Chocolate Cherry Porter
- Gingerbread Spiced Ale
- Citrus IPA
- Rye Pale Ale
- Smoked Porter
- Saison
- Mocha Milk Stout
- Coconut Cream Ale
- Black IPA
- Raspberry Wheat Beer
- Oatmeal Stout

- Lemon Ginger Shandy
- Altbier
- Double IPA
- Milkshake IPA

Classic Lager

Ingredients:

- 8 lbs (3.63 kg) Pilsner malt
- 1 lb (0.45 kg) Munich malt
- 1 oz (28 g) Saaz hops (60 minutes)
- 1 oz (28 g) Saaz hops (15 minutes)
- 1 Whirlfloc tablet (15 minutes)
- 1 packet of lager yeast (e.g., WLP830 or Wyeast 2124)
- 5 gallons (19 liters) of water (for brewing)
- Priming sugar (for bottling)

Instructions:

1. Mashing:

- Heat 3.5 gallons (13 liters) of water to around 165°F (74°C).
- Add crushed grains to a grain bag and steep in the water for 60 minutes at a temperature around 150°F (65.6°C).
- Remove the grain bag and let it drain into the kettle. Sparge with additional water if necessary.

2. Boiling:

- Bring the wort to a boil and add 1 oz of Saaz hops.
- Boil for 45 minutes, then add another 1 oz of Saaz hops and the Whirlfloc tablet.
- Continue boiling for an additional 15 minutes.

3. Cooling and Fermentation:

- Cool the wort quickly using a wort chiller or an ice bath to around 50-55°F (10-13°C).
- Transfer the cooled wort to a sanitized fermenter and top up with water to reach a total volume of 5 gallons (19 liters).
- Aerate the wort and pitch the lager yeast.

4. Lagering:

- Ferment at a temperature of around 50°F (10°C) for the first few days, then slowly lower the temperature to 45°F (7°C).
- Allow the beer to lager for 4-6 weeks.

5. Bottling:

- Once fermentation is complete and the beer has cleared, mix priming sugar into the beer and transfer to sanitized bottles.
- Cap the bottles and allow them to carbonate for at least 2-3 weeks.

6. Conditioning:

- Store the bottled beer in a cool, dark place for a few weeks to allow it to condition and carbonate fully.

7. Enjoy:

- Chill the beer, pour into a glass, and enjoy your classic lager!

Note: Make sure to follow proper sanitation procedures at every step to ensure a clean and contamination-free brew. Adjust the recipe according to your brewing setup and preferences.

Pale Ale

Ingredients:

- 9 lbs (4.08 kg) Pale Ale malt
- 1 lb (0.45 kg) Crystal malt (20L)
- 0.5 lb (0.23 kg) Munich malt
- 1 oz (28 g) Cascade hops (60 minutes)
- 1 oz (28 g) Cascade hops (15 minutes)
- 1 oz (28 g) Cascade hops (5 minutes)
- 1 Whirlfloc tablet (15 minutes)
- 1 packet of American Ale yeast (e.g., Safale US-05 or Wyeast 1056)
- 5 gallons (19 liters) of water (for brewing)
- Priming sugar (for bottling)

Instructions:

1. Mashing:

- Heat 3.5 gallons (13 liters) of water to around 165°F (74°C).
- Add crushed grains to a grain bag and steep in the water for 60 minutes at a temperature around 152°F (67°C).
- Remove the grain bag and let it drain into the kettle. Sparge with additional water if necessary.

2. Boiling:

- Bring the wort to a boil and add 1 oz of Cascade hops.
- Boil for 45 minutes, then add another 1 oz of Cascade hops and the Whirlfloc tablet.
- Add 1 oz of Cascade hops at 5 minutes before the end of the boil.

3. Cooling and Fermentation:

- Cool the wort quickly using a wort chiller or an ice bath to around 68°F (20°C).
- Transfer the cooled wort to a sanitized fermenter and top up with water to reach a total volume of 5 gallons (19 liters).
- Aerate the wort and pitch the American Ale yeast.

4. Fermentation:

- Ferment at a temperature of around 65-70°F (18-21°C) for 1-2 weeks or until fermentation is complete.

5. Bottling:

- Once fermentation is complete and the beer has cleared, mix priming sugar into the beer and transfer to sanitized bottles.
- Cap the bottles and allow them to carbonate for at least 2-3 weeks.

6. Conditioning:

- Store the bottled beer in a cool, dark place for a few weeks to allow it to condition and carbonate fully.

7. Enjoy:

- Chill the beer, pour into a glass, and savor your homemade Pale Ale!

Note: Adjust the recipe according to your brewing setup, hop preferences, and yeast choice. Ensure proper sanitation throughout the brewing process for the best results.

India Pale Ale (IPA)

Ingredients:

- 11 lbs (5 kg) Pale Ale malt
- 1 lb (0.45 kg) Munich malt
- 0.5 lb (0.23 kg) Crystal malt (40L)
- 1 oz (28 g) Columbus hops (60 minutes)
- 1 oz (28 g) Centennial hops (15 minutes)
- 1 oz (28 g) Citra hops (10 minutes)
- 1 oz (28 g) Simcoe hops (5 minutes)
- 1 oz (28 g) Amarillo hops (0 minutes, flameout)
- 1 Whirlfloc tablet (15 minutes)
- 1 packet of American Ale yeast (e.g., Safale US-05 or Wyeast 1056)
- Dry hops: 2 oz (56 g) Citra, 2 oz (56 g) Simcoe, 1 oz (28 g) Amarillo
- 5 gallons (19 liters) of water (for brewing)
- Priming sugar (for bottling)

Instructions:

1. Mashing:

- Heat 3.5 gallons (13 liters) of water to around 165°F (74°C).
- Add crushed grains to a grain bag and steep in the water for 60 minutes at a temperature around 152°F (67°C).
- Remove the grain bag and let it drain into the kettle. Sparge with additional water if necessary.

2. Boiling:

- Bring the wort to a boil and add 1 oz of Columbus hops.
- Boil for 45 minutes, then add 1 oz of Centennial hops and the Whirlfloc tablet.
- Add 1 oz of Citra hops at 10 minutes, 1 oz of Simcoe hops at 5 minutes, and 1 oz of Amarillo hops at flameout.

3. Cooling and Fermentation:

- Cool the wort quickly using a wort chiller or an ice bath to around 68°F (20°C).
- Transfer the cooled wort to a sanitized fermenter and top up with water to reach a total volume of 5 gallons (19 liters).
- Aerate the wort and pitch the American Ale yeast.

4. Dry Hopping:

- After primary fermentation is complete (usually after 1-2 weeks), add the dry hops to the fermenter.
- Let the beer sit on the dry hops for an additional 4-7 days for enhanced aroma.

5. Bottling:

- Once fermentation and dry hopping are complete, mix priming sugar into the beer and transfer to sanitized bottles.
- Cap the bottles and allow them to carbonate for at least 2-3 weeks.

6. Conditioning:

- Store the bottled beer in a cool, dark place for a few weeks to allow it to condition and carbonate fully.

7. Enjoy:

- Chill the beer, pour into a glass, and revel in the hoppy goodness of your homemade IPA!

Note: Adjust the recipe according to your brewing setup, hop preferences, and yeast choice. Ensure proper sanitation throughout the brewing process for the best results.

Stout

Ingredients:

- 9 lbs (4.08 kg) Maris Otter malt
- 1 lb (0.45 kg) Flaked Barley
- 1 lb (0.45 kg) Chocolate malt
- 0.5 lb (0.23 kg) Roasted Barley
- 0.5 lb (0.23 kg) Crystal malt (60L)
- 1 oz (28 g) East Kent Goldings hops (60 minutes)
- 1 Whirlfloc tablet (15 minutes)
- 1 packet of Irish Ale yeast (e.g., Safale S-04 or Wyeast 1084)
- 5 gallons (19 liters) of water (for brewing)
- Priming sugar (for bottling)

Instructions:

1. Mashing:

- Heat 3.5 gallons (13 liters) of water to around 165°F (74°C).
- Add crushed grains to a grain bag and steep in the water for 60 minutes at a temperature around 154°F (68°C).
- Remove the grain bag and let it drain into the kettle. Sparge with additional water if necessary.

2. Boiling:

- Bring the wort to a boil and add 1 oz of East Kent Goldings hops.
- Boil for 45 minutes, then add the Whirlfloc tablet.
- Continue boiling for an additional 15 minutes.

3. Cooling and Fermentation:

- Cool the wort quickly using a wort chiller or an ice bath to around 68°F (20°C).
- Transfer the cooled wort to a sanitized fermenter and top up with water to reach a total volume of 5 gallons (19 liters).
- Aerate the wort and pitch the Irish Ale yeast.

4. Fermentation:

- Ferment at a temperature of around 65-70°F (18-21°C) for 2-3 weeks or until fermentation is complete.

5. Bottling:

- Once fermentation is complete and the beer has cleared, mix priming sugar into the beer and transfer to sanitized bottles.
- Cap the bottles and allow them to carbonate for at least 2-3 weeks.

6. Conditioning:

- Store the bottled beer in a cool, dark place for a few weeks to allow it to condition and carbonate fully.

7. Enjoy:

- Chill the beer, pour into a glass, and savor the rich, roasty flavors of your homemade Stout!

Note: Adjust the recipe according to your brewing setup and preferences. Ensure proper sanitation throughout the brewing process for the best results.

Porter

Ingredients:

- 8 lbs (3.63 kg) Pale Ale malt
- 1 lb (0.45 kg) Munich malt
- 0.75 lb (0.34 kg) Chocolate malt
- 0.5 lb (0.23 kg) Crystal malt (40L)
- 0.25 lb (0.11 kg) Black Patent malt
- 1 oz (28 g) East Kent Goldings hops (60 minutes)
- 1 Whirlfloc tablet (15 minutes)
- 1 packet of English Ale yeast (e.g., Safale S-04 or Wyeast 1968)
- 5 gallons (19 liters) of water (for brewing)
- Priming sugar (for bottling)

Instructions:

1. Mashing:

- Heat 3.5 gallons (13 liters) of water to around 165°F (74°C).
- Add crushed grains to a grain bag and steep in the water for 60 minutes at a temperature around 154°F (68°C).
- Remove the grain bag and let it drain into the kettle. Sparge with additional water if necessary.

2. Boiling:

- Bring the wort to a boil and add 1 oz of East Kent Goldings hops.
- Boil for 45 minutes, then add the Whirlfloc tablet.
- Continue boiling for an additional 15 minutes.

3. Cooling and Fermentation:

- Cool the wort quickly using a wort chiller or an ice bath to around 68°F (20°C).
- Transfer the cooled wort to a sanitized fermenter and top up with water to reach a total volume of 5 gallons (19 liters).
- Aerate the wort and pitch the English Ale yeast.

4. Fermentation:

- Ferment at a temperature of around 65-70°F (18-21°C) for 2-3 weeks or until fermentation is complete.

5. Bottling:

- Once fermentation is complete and the beer has cleared, mix priming sugar into the beer and transfer to sanitized bottles.
- Cap the bottles and allow them to carbonate for at least 2-3 weeks.

6. Conditioning:

- Store the bottled beer in a cool, dark place for a few weeks to allow it to condition and carbonate fully.

7. Enjoy:

- Chill the beer, pour into a glass, and appreciate the smooth, malt-forward character of your homemade Porter!

Note: Adjust the recipe according to your brewing setup and preferences. Ensure proper sanitation throughout the brewing process for the best results.

Belgian Witbier

Ingredients:

- 5 lbs (2.27 kg) Pilsner malt
- 4 lbs (1.81 kg) Wheat malt
- 0.5 lb (0.23 kg) Flaked oats
- 1 oz (28 g) Saaz hops (60 minutes)
- 1 oz (28 g) Sweet orange peel (5 minutes)
- 1 oz (28 g) Crushed coriander seeds (5 minutes)
- 0.5 oz (14 g) Saaz hops (5 minutes)
- 1 Whirlfloc tablet (15 minutes)
- 1 packet of Belgian Witbier yeast (e.g., Wyeast 3944 or Safbrew WB-06)
- 5 gallons (19 liters) of water (for brewing)
- Priming sugar (for bottling)

Instructions:

1. Mashing:

- Heat 3.5 gallons (13 liters) of water to around 165°F (74°C).
- Add crushed grains to a grain bag and steep in the water for 60 minutes at a temperature around 152°F (67°C).
- Remove the grain bag and let it drain into the kettle. Sparge with additional water if necessary.

2. Boiling:

- Bring the wort to a boil and add 1 oz of Saaz hops.
- Boil for 55 minutes, then add the Whirlfloc tablet, sweet orange peel, crushed coriander seeds, and 0.5 oz of Saaz hops.
- Continue boiling for an additional 5 minutes.

3. Cooling and Fermentation:

- Cool the wort quickly using a wort chiller or an ice bath to around 68°F (20°C).

- Transfer the cooled wort to a sanitized fermenter and top up with water to reach a total volume of 5 gallons (19 liters).
- Aerate the wort and pitch the Belgian Witbier yeast.

4. Fermentation:

- Ferment at a temperature of around 65-70°F (18-21°C) for 1-2 weeks or until fermentation is complete.

5. Bottling:

- Once fermentation is complete and the beer has cleared, mix priming sugar into the beer and transfer to sanitized bottles.
- Cap the bottles and allow them to carbonate for at least 2-3 weeks.

6. Conditioning:

- Store the bottled beer in a cool, dark place for a few weeks to allow it to condition and carbonate fully.

7. Enjoy:

- Chill the beer, pour into a glass, and savor the light and citrusy flavors of your homemade Belgian Witbier!

Note: Adjust the recipe according to your brewing setup and preferences. Ensure proper sanitation throughout the brewing process for the best results.

Hefeweizen

Ingredients:

- 5 lbs (2.27 kg) Wheat malt
- 5 lbs (2.27 kg) Pilsner malt
- 0.5 lb (0.23 kg) Munich malt
- 0.5 oz (14 g) Hallertau hops (60 minutes)
- 1 Whirlfloc tablet (15 minutes)
- 1 packet of Hefeweizen yeast (e.g., Wyeast 3068 or Safbrew WB-06)
- 5 gallons (19 liters) of water (for brewing)
- Priming sugar (for bottling)

Instructions:

1. Mashing:

- Heat 3.5 gallons (13 liters) of water to around 165°F (74°C).
- Add crushed grains to a grain bag and steep in the water for 60 minutes at a temperature around 152°F (67°C).
- Remove the grain bag and let it drain into the kettle. Sparge with additional water if necessary.

2. Boiling:

- Bring the wort to a boil and add 0.5 oz of Hallertau hops.
- Boil for 45 minutes, then add the Whirlfloc tablet.
- Continue boiling for an additional 15 minutes.

3. Cooling and Fermentation:

- Cool the wort quickly using a wort chiller or an ice bath to around 68°F (20°C).
- Transfer the cooled wort to a sanitized fermenter and top up with water to reach a total volume of 5 gallons (19 liters).
- Aerate the wort and pitch the Hefeweizen yeast.

4. Fermentation:

- Ferment at a temperature of around 62-72°F (17-22°C) for 1-2 weeks or until fermentation is complete.

- Hefeweizen yeast tends to produce more esters and phenols at higher temperatures, contributing to the beer's characteristic fruity and spicy notes. Consider fermenting on the warmer end of the range for a more pronounced yeast character.

5. Bottling:

- Once fermentation is complete and the beer has cleared, mix priming sugar into the beer and transfer to sanitized bottles.
- Cap the bottles and allow them to carbonate for at least 2-3 weeks.

6. Conditioning:

- Store the bottled beer in a cool, dark place for a few weeks to allow it to condition and carbonate fully.

7. Enjoy:

- Chill the beer, pour into a tall glass, and appreciate the fruity and spicy flavors of your homemade Hefeweizen!

Note: Adjust the recipe according to your brewing setup and preferences. Ensure proper sanitation throughout the brewing process for the best results.

Pilsner

Ingredients:

- 9 lbs (4.08 kg) Pilsner malt
- 1 lb (0.45 kg) Munich malt
- 1 oz (28 g) Saaz hops (60 minutes)
- 1 oz (28 g) Saaz hops (30 minutes)
- 1 oz (28 g) Saaz hops (15 minutes)
- 1 Whirlfloc tablet (15 minutes)
- 1 packet of Czech Pilsner yeast (e.g., Wyeast 2278 or Saflager W-34/70)
- 5 gallons (19 liters) of water (for brewing)
- Priming sugar (for bottling)

Instructions:

1. Mashing:

- Heat 3.5 gallons (13 liters) of water to around 165°F (74°C).
- Add crushed grains to a grain bag and steep in the water for 60 minutes at a temperature around 150°F (65.6°C).
- Remove the grain bag and let it drain into the kettle. Sparge with additional water if necessary.

2. Boiling:

- Bring the wort to a boil and add 1 oz of Saaz hops.
- Boil for 30 minutes, then add another 1 oz of Saaz hops.
- Add 1 oz of Saaz hops and the Whirlfloc tablet at 15 minutes.

3. Cooling and Fermentation:

- Cool the wort quickly using a wort chiller or an ice bath to around 48-52°F (9-11°C).
- Transfer the cooled wort to a sanitized fermenter and top up with water to reach a total volume of 5 gallons (19 liters).
- Aerate the wort and pitch the Czech Pilsner yeast.

4. Fermentation:

- Ferment at a temperature of around 48-52°F (9-11°C) for 3-4 weeks. Pilsners benefit from a long, cold fermentation for a clean and crisp profile.

5. Bottling:

- Once fermentation is complete and the beer has cleared, mix priming sugar into the beer and transfer to sanitized bottles.
- Cap the bottles and allow them to carbonate for at least 4-6 weeks. Pilsners often require extended conditioning for optimal flavor.

6. Conditioning:

- Store the bottled beer in a cool, dark place for an extended period to allow it to condition and carbonate fully. Longer conditioning times will enhance the beer's clarity and flavor.

7. Enjoy:

- Chill the beer, pour into a tall, thin glass, and savor the clean and refreshing taste of your homemade Pilsner!

Note: Adjust the recipe according to your brewing setup and preferences. Ensure proper sanitation throughout the brewing process for the best results.

Brown Ale

Ingredients:

- 8 lbs (3.63 kg) Maris Otter malt
- 1 lb (0.45 kg) Crystal malt (40L)
- 0.5 lb (0.23 kg) Chocolate malt
- 0.5 lb (0.23 kg) Munich malt
- 0.25 lb (0.11 kg) Victory malt
- 1 oz (28 g) East Kent Goldings hops (60 minutes)
- 0.5 oz (14 g) East Kent Goldings hops (15 minutes)
- 1 Whirlfloc tablet (15 minutes)
- 1 packet of English Ale yeast (e.g., Safale S-04 or Wyeast 1968)
- 5 gallons (19 liters) of water (for brewing)
- Priming sugar (for bottling)

Instructions:

1. Mashing:

- Heat 3.5 gallons (13 liters) of water to around 165°F (74°C).
- Add crushed grains to a grain bag and steep in the water for 60 minutes at a temperature around 155°F (68°C).
- Remove the grain bag and let it drain into the kettle. Sparge with additional water if necessary.

2. Boiling:

- Bring the wort to a boil and add 1 oz of East Kent Goldings hops.
- Boil for 45 minutes, then add the Whirlfloc tablet and 0.5 oz of East Kent Goldings hops.
- Continue boiling for an additional 15 minutes.

3. Cooling and Fermentation:

- Cool the wort quickly using a wort chiller or an ice bath to around 68°F (20°C).
- Transfer the cooled wort to a sanitized fermenter and top up with water to reach a total volume of 5 gallons (19 liters).
- Aerate the wort and pitch the English Ale yeast.

4. Fermentation:

- Ferment at a temperature of around 65-70°F (18-21°C) for 2-3 weeks or until fermentation is complete.

5. Bottling:

- Once fermentation is complete and the beer has cleared, mix priming sugar into the beer and transfer to sanitized bottles.
- Cap the bottles and allow them to carbonate for at least 2-3 weeks.

6. Conditioning:

- Store the bottled beer in a cool, dark place for a few weeks to allow it to condition and carbonate fully.

7. Enjoy:

- Chill the beer, pour into a glass, and savor the malt-forward goodness of your homemade Brown Ale!

Note: Adjust the recipe according to your brewing setup and preferences. Ensure proper sanitation throughout the brewing process for the best results.

Scottish Ale

Ingredients:

- 8 lbs (3.63 kg) Maris Otter malt
- 1 lb (0.45 kg) Munich malt
- 1 lb (0.45 kg) Crystal malt (60L)
- 0.5 lb (0.23 kg) Special B malt
- 0.25 lb (0.11 kg) Chocolate malt
- 0.5 oz (14 g) East Kent Goldings hops (60 minutes)
- 0.5 oz (14 g) East Kent Goldings hops (30 minutes)
- 1 Whirlfloc tablet (15 minutes)
- 1 packet of Scottish Ale yeast (e.g., Wyeast 1728 or Safale S-04)
- 5 gallons (19 liters) of water (for brewing)
- Priming sugar (for bottling)

Instructions:

1. Mashing:

- Heat 3.5 gallons (13 liters) of water to around 165°F (74°C).
- Add crushed grains to a grain bag and steep in the water for 60 minutes at a temperature around 154°F (68°C).
- Remove the grain bag and let it drain into the kettle. Sparge with additional water if necessary.

2. Boiling:

- Bring the wort to a boil and add 0.5 oz of East Kent Goldings hops.
- Boil for 30 minutes, then add another 0.5 oz of East Kent Goldings hops.
- Add the Whirlfloc tablet at 15 minutes.

3. Cooling and Fermentation:

- Cool the wort quickly using a wort chiller or an ice bath to around 68°F (20°C).
- Transfer the cooled wort to a sanitized fermenter and top up with water to reach a total volume of 5 gallons (19 liters).
- Aerate the wort and pitch the Scottish Ale yeast.

4. Fermentation:

- Ferment at a temperature of around 60-65°F (15-18°C) for 2-3 weeks or until fermentation is complete.

5. Bottling:

- Once fermentation is complete and the beer has cleared, mix priming sugar into the beer and transfer to sanitized bottles.
- Cap the bottles and allow them to carbonate for at least 2-3 weeks.

6. Conditioning:

- Store the bottled beer in a cool, dark place for a few weeks to allow it to condition and carbonate fully.

7. Enjoy:

- Chill the beer, pour into a glass, and savor the malt-forward and caramel notes of your homemade Scottish Ale!

Note: Adjust the recipe according to your brewing setup and preferences. Ensure proper sanitation throughout the brewing process for the best results.

American Amber Ale

Ingredients:

- 9 lbs (4.08 kg) Pale Ale malt
- 1 lb (0.45 kg) Crystal malt (40L)
- 0.5 lb (0.23 kg) Munich malt
- 0.25 lb (0.11 kg) Victory malt
- 0.25 lb (0.11 kg) Special B malt
- 1 oz (28 g) Cascade hops (60 minutes)
- 1 oz (28 g) Cascade hops (15 minutes)
- 0.5 oz (14 g) Cascade hops (5 minutes)
- 1 Whirlfloc tablet (15 minutes)
- 1 packet of American Ale yeast (e.g., Safale US-05 or Wyeast 1056)
- 5 gallons (19 liters) of water (for brewing)
- Priming sugar (for bottling)

Instructions:

1. Mashing:

- Heat 3.5 gallons (13 liters) of water to around 165°F (74°C).
- Add crushed grains to a grain bag and steep in the water for 60 minutes at a temperature around 152°F (67°C).
- Remove the grain bag and let it drain into the kettle. Sparge with additional water if necessary.

2. Boiling:

- Bring the wort to a boil and add 1 oz of Cascade hops.
- Boil for 45 minutes, then add another 1 oz of Cascade hops and the Whirlfloc tablet.
- Add 0.5 oz of Cascade hops at 5 minutes before the end of the boil.

3. Cooling and Fermentation:

- Cool the wort quickly using a wort chiller or an ice bath to around 68°F (20°C).

- Transfer the cooled wort to a sanitized fermenter and top up with water to reach a total volume of 5 gallons (19 liters).
- Aerate the wort and pitch the American Ale yeast.

4. Fermentation:

- Ferment at a temperature of around 65-70°F (18-21°C) for 2-3 weeks or until fermentation is complete.

5. Bottling:

- Once fermentation is complete and the beer has cleared, mix priming sugar into the beer and transfer to sanitized bottles.
- Cap the bottles and allow them to carbonate for at least 2-3 weeks.

6. Conditioning:

- Store the bottled beer in a cool, dark place for a few weeks to allow it to condition and carbonate fully.

7. Enjoy:

- Chill the beer, pour into a glass, and savor the balanced malt and hop flavors of your homemade American Amber Ale!

Note: Adjust the recipe according to your brewing setup and preferences. Ensure proper sanitation throughout the brewing process for the best results.

Irish Red Ale

Ingredients:

- 8 lbs (3.63 kg) Maris Otter malt
- 1 lb (0.45 kg) Crystal malt (40L)
- 0.5 lb (0.23 kg) Munich malt
- 0.25 lb (0.11 kg) Melanoidin malt
- 0.5 oz (14 g) East Kent Goldings hops (60 minutes)
- 0.5 oz (14 g) East Kent Goldings hops (15 minutes)
- 1 Whirlfloc tablet (15 minutes)
- 1 packet of Irish Ale yeast (e.g., Wyeast 1084 or Safale S-04)
- 5 gallons (19 liters) of water (for brewing)
- Priming sugar (for bottling)

Instructions:

1. Mashing:

- Heat 3.5 gallons (13 liters) of water to around 165°F (74°C).
- Add crushed grains to a grain bag and steep in the water for 60 minutes at a temperature around 154°F (68°C).
- Remove the grain bag and let it drain into the kettle. Sparge with additional water if necessary.

2. Boiling:

- Bring the wort to a boil and add 0.5 oz of East Kent Goldings hops.
- Boil for 45 minutes, then add the Whirlfloc tablet and another 0.5 oz of East Kent Goldings hops.
- Continue boiling for an additional 15 minutes.

3. Cooling and Fermentation:

- Cool the wort quickly using a wort chiller or an ice bath to around 68°F (20°C).
- Transfer the cooled wort to a sanitized fermenter and top up with water to reach a total volume of 5 gallons (19 liters).
- Aerate the wort and pitch the Irish Ale yeast.

4. Fermentation:

- Ferment at a temperature of around 65-70°F (18-21°C) for 2-3 weeks or until fermentation is complete.

5. Bottling:

- Once fermentation is complete and the beer has cleared, mix priming sugar into the beer and transfer to sanitized bottles.
- Cap the bottles and allow them to carbonate for at least 2-3 weeks.

6. Conditioning:

- Store the bottled beer in a cool, dark place for a few weeks to allow it to condition and carbonate fully.

7. Enjoy:

- Chill the beer, pour into a glass, and savor the malty sweetness and balanced bitterness of your homemade Irish Red Ale!

Note: Adjust the recipe according to your brewing setup and preferences. Ensure proper sanitation throughout the brewing process for the best results.

Kölsch

Ingredients:

- 8 lbs (3.63 kg) Pilsner malt
- 1 lb (0.45 kg) Vienna malt
- 0.5 lb (0.23 kg) Wheat malt
- 1 oz (28 g) Hallertau hops (60 minutes)
- 0.5 oz (14 g) Hallertau hops (15 minutes)
- 1 Whirlfloc tablet (15 minutes)
- 1 packet of Kölsch yeast (e.g., Wyeast 2565 or Safale K-97)
- 5 gallons (19 liters) of water (for brewing)
- Priming sugar (for bottling)

Instructions:

1. Mashing:

- Heat 3.5 gallons (13 liters) of water to around 165°F (74°C).
- Add crushed grains to a grain bag and steep in the water for 60 minutes at a temperature around 150°F (65.6°C).
- Remove the grain bag and let it drain into the kettle. Sparge with additional water if necessary.

2. Boiling:

- Bring the wort to a boil and add 1 oz of Hallertau hops.
- Boil for 45 minutes, then add the Whirlfloc tablet and 0.5 oz of Hallertau hops.
- Continue boiling for an additional 15 minutes.

3. Cooling and Fermentation:

- Cool the wort quickly using a wort chiller or an ice bath to around 60-65°F (15-18°C).
- Transfer the cooled wort to a sanitized fermenter and top up with water to reach a total volume of 5 gallons (19 liters).
- Aerate the wort and pitch the Kölsch yeast.

4. Fermentation:

- Ferment at a temperature of around 60-65°F (15-18°C) for 2-3 weeks or until fermentation is complete.
- Kölsch yeast works best at cooler fermentation temperatures to produce a clean and crisp profile.

5. Bottling:

- Once fermentation is complete and the beer has cleared, mix priming sugar into the beer and transfer to sanitized bottles.
- Cap the bottles and allow them to carbonate for at least 2-3 weeks.

6. Conditioning:

- Store the bottled beer in a cool, dark place for a few weeks to allow it to condition and carbonate fully.

7. Enjoy:

- Chill the beer, pour into a Kölsch glass, and relish the refreshing, crisp taste of your homemade Kölsch!

Note: Adjust the recipe according to your brewing setup and preferences. Ensure proper sanitation throughout the brewing process for the best results.

Belgian Dubbel

Ingredients:

- 8 lbs (3.63 kg) Belgian Pilsner malt
- 1 lb (0.45 kg) Munich malt
- 1 lb (0.45 kg) Special B malt
- 0.5 lb (0.23 kg) Aromatic malt
- 0.5 lb (0.23 kg) Belgian Candi Sugar (Dark)
- 0.25 lb (0.11 kg) Belgian Chocolate malt
- 1 oz (28 g) Styrian Goldings hops (60 minutes)
- 0.5 oz (14 g) Saaz hops (15 minutes)
- 1 Whirlfloc tablet (15 minutes)
- 0.5 oz (14 g) Saaz hops (5 minutes)
- Belgian Abbey Ale yeast (e.g., Wyeast 1214 or Safbrew T-58)
- 5 gallons (19 liters) of water (for brewing)
- Priming sugar (for bottling)

Instructions:

1. Mashing:

- Heat 3.5 gallons (13 liters) of water to around 165°F (74°C).
- Add crushed grains to a grain bag and steep in the water for 60 minutes at a temperature around 150°F (65.6°C).
- Remove the grain bag and let it drain into the kettle. Sparge with additional water if necessary.

2. Boiling:

- Bring the wort to a boil and add 1 oz of Styrian Goldings hops.
- Boil for 45 minutes, then add the Whirlfloc tablet and 0.5 oz of Saaz hops.
- Continue boiling for an additional 10 minutes, then add the remaining 0.5 oz of Saaz hops.

3. Cooling and Fermentation:

- Cool the wort quickly using a wort chiller or an ice bath to around 68°F (20°C).
- Transfer the cooled wort to a sanitized fermenter and top up with water to reach a total volume of 5 gallons (19 liters).

- Aerate the wort and pitch the Belgian Abbey Ale yeast.

4. Fermentation:

- Ferment at a temperature of around 65-75°F (18-24°C) for 2-3 weeks or until fermentation is complete.
- Belgian Dubbels often benefit from higher fermentation temperatures to enhance the yeast character.

5. Bottling:

- Once fermentation is complete and the beer has cleared, mix priming sugar into the beer and transfer to sanitized bottles.
- Cap the bottles and allow them to carbonate for at least 2-4 weeks.

6. Conditioning:

- Store the bottled beer in a cool, dark place for several weeks to allow it to condition and carbonate fully.

7. Enjoy:

- Chill the beer, pour into a goblet or chalice, and appreciate the rich maltiness and complex flavors of your homemade Belgian Dubbel!

Note: Adjust the recipe according to your brewing setup and preferences. Ensure proper sanitation throughout the brewing process for the best results.

Tripel

Ingredients:

- 10 lbs (4.54 kg) Belgian Pilsner malt
- 1 lb (0.45 kg) Munich malt
- 0.5 lb (0.23 kg) Belgian Candi Sugar (Light)
- 1 oz (28 g) Saaz hops (60 minutes)
- 0.5 oz (14 g) Styrian Goldings hops (15 minutes)
- 1 Whirlfloc tablet (15 minutes)
- 0.5 oz (14 g) Saaz hops (5 minutes)
- Belgian Abbey Ale yeast (e.g., Wyeast 1214 or Safbrew T-58)
- 5 gallons (19 liters) of water (for brewing)
- Priming sugar (for bottling)

Instructions:

1. Mashing:

- Heat 3.5 gallons (13 liters) of water to around 165°F (74°C).
- Add crushed grains to a grain bag and steep in the water for 60 minutes at a temperature around 148-150°F (64-66°C).
- Remove the grain bag and let it drain into the kettle. Sparge with additional water if necessary.

2. Boiling:

- Bring the wort to a boil and add 1 oz of Saaz hops.
- Boil for 45 minutes, then add the Whirlfloc tablet and 0.5 oz of Styrian Goldings hops.
- Continue boiling for an additional 10 minutes, then add 0.5 oz of Saaz hops.

3. Adding Candi Sugar:

- Add the Belgian Candi Sugar to the boil during the last 10 minutes.

4. Cooling and Fermentation:

- Cool the wort quickly using a wort chiller or an ice bath to around 68°F (20°C).
- Transfer the cooled wort to a sanitized fermenter and top up with water to reach a total volume of 5 gallons (19 liters).
- Aerate the wort and pitch the Belgian Abbey Ale yeast.

5. Fermentation:

- Ferment at a temperature of around 68-75°F (20-24°C) for 2-3 weeks or until fermentation is complete.
- Tripels often benefit from warmer fermentation temperatures to encourage the development of esters and phenols.

6. Bottling:

- Once fermentation is complete and the beer has cleared, mix priming sugar into the beer and transfer to sanitized bottles.
- Cap the bottles and allow them to carbonate for at least 2-4 weeks.

7. Conditioning:

- Store the bottled beer in a cool, dark place for several weeks to allow it to condition and carbonate fully.

8. Enjoy:

- Chill the beer, pour into a goblet or chalice, and savor the strength and complexity of your homemade Belgian Tripel!

Note: Adjust the recipe according to your brewing setup and preferences. Ensure proper sanitation throughout the brewing process for the best results.

Baltic Porter

Ingredients:

- 10 lbs (4.54 kg) Munich malt
- 4 lbs (1.81 kg) Pilsner malt
- 1 lb (0.45 kg) Chocolate malt
- 0.5 lb (0.23 kg) Carafa Special III malt
- 0.5 lb (0.23 kg) Crystal malt (40L)
- 1 lb (0.45 kg) Dark Munich malt
- 1 oz (28 g) Hallertau hops (60 minutes)
- 1 Whirlfloc tablet (15 minutes)
- 1 packet of Baltic Lager yeast (e.g., Wyeast 2278 or Saflager W-34/70)
- 5 gallons (19 liters) of water (for brewing)
- Priming sugar (for bottling)

Instructions:

1. Mashing:

- Heat 3.5 gallons (13 liters) of water to around 165°F (74°C).
- Add crushed grains to a grain bag and steep in the water for 60 minutes at a temperature around 154°F (68°C).
- Remove the grain bag and let it drain into the kettle. Sparge with additional water if necessary.

2. Boiling:

- Bring the wort to a boil and add 1 oz of Hallertau hops.
- Boil for 45 minutes, then add the Whirlfloc tablet.
- Continue boiling for an additional 15 minutes.

3. Cooling and Fermentation:

- Cool the wort quickly using a wort chiller or an ice bath to around 50-55°F (10-13°C).
- Transfer the cooled wort to a sanitized fermenter and top up with water to reach a total volume of 5 gallons (19 liters).
- Aerate the wort and pitch the Baltic Lager yeast.

4. Fermentation:

- Ferment at a temperature of around 50-55°F (10-13°C) for 4-6 weeks. Baltic Porters benefit from an extended lagering period for smoothness and flavor development.

5. Bottling:

- Once fermentation is complete and the beer has cleared, mix priming sugar into the beer and transfer to sanitized bottles.
- Cap the bottles and allow them to carbonate for at least 6-8 weeks.

6. Conditioning:

- Lager the bottled beer in a cool environment for an extended period, ideally at temperatures around 35-45°F (2-7°C), for several months.

7. Enjoy:

- Chill the beer, pour into a snifter or tulip glass, and savor the rich maltiness and complexity of your homemade Baltic Porter!

Note: Adjust the recipe according to your brewing setup and preferences. Ensure proper sanitation throughout the brewing process for the best results.

American Wheat Beer

Ingredients:

- 5 lbs (2.27 kg) American 2-row pale malt
- 4 lbs (1.81 kg) White wheat malt
- 0.5 lb (0.23 kg) Carapils malt
- 0.5 oz (14 g) Cascade hops (60 minutes)
- 0.5 oz (14 g) Cascade hops (15 minutes)
- 1 Whirlfloc tablet (15 minutes)
- 0.5 oz (14 g) Cascade hops (5 minutes)
- 1 packet of American Wheat Beer yeast (e.g., Safale US-05 or Wyeast 1010)
- 5 gallons (19 liters) of water (for brewing)
- Priming sugar (for bottling)

Instructions:

1. Mashing:

- Heat 3.5 gallons (13 liters) of water to around 165°F (74°C).
- Add crushed grains to a grain bag and steep in the water for 60 minutes at a temperature around 152°F (67°C).
- Remove the grain bag and let it drain into the kettle. Sparge with additional water if necessary.

2. Boiling:

- Bring the wort to a boil and add 0.5 oz of Cascade hops.
- Boil for 45 minutes, then add the Whirlfloc tablet and another 0.5 oz of Cascade hops.
- Continue boiling for an additional 10 minutes, then add the remaining 0.5 oz of Cascade hops.

3. Cooling and Fermentation:

- Cool the wort quickly using a wort chiller or an ice bath to around 68°F (20°C).
- Transfer the cooled wort to a sanitized fermenter and top up with water to reach a total volume of 5 gallons (19 liters).
- Aerate the wort and pitch the American Wheat Beer yeast.

4. Fermentation:

- Ferment at a temperature of around 65-70°F (18-21°C) for 2-3 weeks or until fermentation is complete.

5. Bottling:

- Once fermentation is complete and the beer has cleared, mix priming sugar into the beer and transfer to sanitized bottles.
- Cap the bottles and allow them to carbonate for at least 2-3 weeks.

6. Conditioning:

- Store the bottled beer in a cool, dark place for a few weeks to allow it to condition and carbonate fully.

7. Enjoy:

- Chill the beer, pour into a pint glass, and relish the light and refreshing taste of your homemade American Wheat Beer!

Note: Adjust the recipe according to your brewing setup and preferences. Ensure proper sanitation throughout the brewing process for the best results.

Cream Ale

Ingredients:

- 6 lbs (2.72 kg) American 2-row pale malt
- 2 lbs (0.91 kg) Flaked corn
- 0.5 lb (0.23 kg) Munich malt
- 0.5 oz (14 g) Cluster hops (60 minutes)
- 0.5 oz (14 g) Saaz hops (15 minutes)
- 1 Whirlfloc tablet (15 minutes)
- 0.5 oz (14 g) Saaz hops (5 minutes)
- American Ale yeast (e.g., Safale US-05 or Wyeast 1056)
- 5 gallons (19 liters) of water (for brewing)
- Priming sugar (for bottling)

Instructions:

1. Mashing:

- Heat 3.5 gallons (13 liters) of water to around 165°F (74°C).
- Add crushed grains to a grain bag and steep in the water for 60 minutes at a temperature around 150°F (65.6°C).
- Remove the grain bag and let it drain into the kettle. Sparge with additional water if necessary.

2. Boiling:

- Bring the wort to a boil and add 0.5 oz of Cluster hops.
- Boil for 45 minutes, then add the Whirlfloc tablet and 0.5 oz of Saaz hops.
- Continue boiling for an additional 10 minutes, then add the remaining 0.5 oz of Saaz hops.

3. Cooling and Fermentation:

- Cool the wort quickly using a wort chiller or an ice bath to around 68°F (20°C).
- Transfer the cooled wort to a sanitized fermenter and top up with water to reach a total volume of 5 gallons (19 liters).
- Aerate the wort and pitch the American Ale yeast.

4. Fermentation:

- Ferment at a temperature of around 60-65°F (15-18°C) for 2-3 weeks or until fermentation is complete.

5. Bottling:

- Once fermentation is complete and the beer has cleared, mix priming sugar into the beer and transfer to sanitized bottles.
- Cap the bottles and allow them to carbonate for at least 2-3 weeks.

6. Conditioning:

- Store the bottled beer in a cool, dark place for a few weeks to allow it to condition and carbonate fully.

7. Enjoy:

- Chill the beer, pour into a pint glass, and savor the light and smooth flavor of your homemade Cream Ale!

Note: Adjust the recipe according to your brewing setup and preferences. Ensure proper sanitation throughout the brewing process for the best results.

Barleywine

Ingredients:

- 14 lbs (6.35 kg) Maris Otter malt
- 1 lb (0.45 kg) Crystal malt (60L)
- 1 lb (0.45 kg) Crystal malt (120L)
- 1 lb (0.45 kg) Munich malt
- 1 lb (0.45 kg) Melanoidin malt
- 2 oz (56 g) East Kent Goldings hops (60 minutes)
- 1 oz (28 g) East Kent Goldings hops (30 minutes)
- 1 Whirlfloc tablet (15 minutes)
- English Ale yeast (e.g., Wyeast 1968 or Safale S-04)
- 5 gallons (19 liters) of water (for brewing)
- Priming sugar (for bottling)

Instructions:

1. Mashing:

- Heat 4.5 gallons (17 liters) of water to around 165°F (74°C).
- Add crushed grains to a grain bag and steep in the water for 60 minutes at a temperature around 154°F (68°C).
- Remove the grain bag and let it drain into the kettle. Sparge with additional water if necessary.

2. Boiling:

- Bring the wort to a boil and add 2 oz of East Kent Goldings hops.
- Boil for 30 minutes, then add 1 oz of East Kent Goldings hops and the Whirlfloc tablet.
- Continue boiling for an additional 30 minutes.

3. Cooling and Fermentation:

- Cool the wort quickly using a wort chiller or an ice bath to around 68°F (20°C).
- Transfer the cooled wort to a sanitized fermenter and top up with water to reach a total volume of 5 gallons (19 liters).
- Aerate the wort and pitch the English Ale yeast.

4. Fermentation:

- Ferment at a temperature of around 65-70°F (18-21°C) for 2-3 weeks or until fermentation is complete.

5. Bottling:

- Once fermentation is complete and the beer has cleared, mix priming sugar into the beer and transfer to sanitized bottles.
- Cap the bottles and allow them to carbonate for at least 2-3 months. Barleywines benefit from extended aging.

6. Conditioning:

- Store the bottled beer in a cool, dark place for several months to allow it to condition and mature. Barleywines can improve with age.

7. Enjoy:

- Chill the beer, pour into a snifter or tulip glass, and savor the complex malt flavors and warming alcohol of your homemade English Barleywine!

Note: Adjust the recipe according to your brewing setup and preferences. Ensure proper sanitation throughout the brewing process for the best results.

English Bitter

Ingredients:

- 8 lbs (3.63 kg) Maris Otter malt
- 0.5 lb (0.23 kg) Crystal malt (40L)
- 0.25 lb (0.11 kg) Special B malt
- 1 oz (28 g) East Kent Goldings hops (60 minutes)
- 0.5 oz (14 g) East Kent Goldings hops (15 minutes)
- 0.5 oz (14 g) East Kent Goldings hops (5 minutes)
- 1 Whirlfloc tablet (15 minutes)
- English Ale yeast (e.g., Wyeast 1968 or Safale S-04)
- 5 gallons (19 liters) of water (for brewing)
- Priming sugar (for bottling)

Instructions:

1. Mashing:

- Heat 3.5 gallons (13 liters) of water to around 165°F (74°C).
- Add crushed grains to a grain bag and steep in the water for 60 minutes at a temperature around 152°F (67°C).
- Remove the grain bag and let it drain into the kettle. Sparge with additional water if necessary.

2. Boiling:

- Bring the wort to a boil and add 1 oz of East Kent Goldings hops.
- Boil for 45 minutes, then add the Whirlfloc tablet and 0.5 oz of East Kent Goldings hops.
- Continue boiling for an additional 10 minutes, then add the remaining 0.5 oz of East Kent Goldings hops.

3. Cooling and Fermentation:

- Cool the wort quickly using a wort chiller or an ice bath to around 68°F (20°C).
- Transfer the cooled wort to a sanitized fermenter and top up with water to reach a total volume of 5 gallons (19 liters).
- Aerate the wort and pitch the English Ale yeast.

4. Fermentation:

- Ferment at a temperature of around 65-70°F (18-21°C) for 1-2 weeks or until fermentation is complete.

5. Bottling:

- Once fermentation is complete and the beer has cleared, mix priming sugar into the beer and transfer to sanitized bottles.
- Cap the bottles and allow them to carbonate for at least 2-3 weeks.

6. Conditioning:

- Store the bottled beer in a cool, dark place for a few weeks to allow it to condition and carbonate fully.

7. Enjoy:

- Chill the beer, pour into a pint glass, and appreciate the balanced malt and hop character of your homemade English Bitter!

Note: Adjust the recipe according to your brewing setup and preferences. Ensure proper sanitation throughout the brewing process for the best results.

Berliner Weisse

Ingredients:

- 5 lbs (2.27 kg) German Pilsner malt
- 3 lbs (1.36 kg) German Wheat malt
- 1 oz (28 g) Hallertau hops (60 minutes)
- Berliner Weisse yeast blend or Lactobacillus culture
- German Ale yeast (e.g., Wyeast 1007 or Safale K-97)
- 5 gallons (19 liters) of water (for brewing)
- Priming sugar (for bottling)

Instructions:

1. Mashing:

- Heat 3.5 gallons (13 liters) of water to around 150°F (65.6°C).
- Add crushed grains to a grain bag and steep in the water for 60 minutes at a temperature around 148-150°F (64-66°C).
- Remove the grain bag and let it drain into the kettle. Sparge with additional water if necessary.

2. Boiling:

- Bring the wort to a boil and add 1 oz of Hallertau hops.
- Boil for 60 minutes. Berliner Weisse is traditionally low in hop bitterness, so keep the hop addition minimal.

3. Cooling and Souring:

- Cool the wort to around 110°F (43°C).
- Introduce the Berliner Weisse yeast blend or a Lactobacillus culture to initiate souring. You can do this by adding a small amount of uncrushed grain, using a commercial Lactobacillus culture, or by utilizing a sour mash technique.
- Allow the wort to sour for 24-48 hours, tasting periodically until the desired level of sourness is achieved.

4. Boiling (Again):

- Bring the soured wort back to a boil for 15 minutes to halt the souring process.

5. Cooling and Fermentation:

- Cool the wort to around 68°F (20°C).
- Transfer the cooled wort to a sanitized fermenter and top up with water to reach a total volume of 5 gallons (19 liters).
- Aerate the wort and pitch the German Ale yeast.

6. Fermentation:

- Ferment at a temperature of around 68-72°F (20-22°C) for 2-3 weeks or until fermentation is complete.

7. Bottling:

- Once fermentation is complete, mix priming sugar into the beer and transfer to sanitized bottles.
- Cap the bottles and allow them to carbonate for 2-3 weeks.

8. Conditioning:

- Berliner Weisse is often enjoyed fresh, but you can age it for a short period to let the flavors meld.

9. Enjoy:

- Chill the beer, pour into a traditional Berliner Weisse glass, and relish the tart and refreshing taste of your homemade Berliner Weisse!

Note: Adjust the recipe according to your brewing setup and preferences. Ensure proper sanitation throughout the brewing process for the best results.

Pumpkin Ale

Ingredients:

- 8 lbs (3.63 kg) Pale malt
- 1 lb (0.45 kg) Munich malt
- 1 lb (0.45 kg) Caramel/Crystal malt (40L)
- 0.5 lb (0.23 kg) Victory malt
- 1.5 lbs (0.68 kg) Pumpkin puree (canned or freshly roasted)
- 0.5 oz (14 g) East Kent Goldings hops (60 minutes)
- 1 tsp Pumpkin Pie Spice (15 minutes)
- 1 Whirlfloc tablet (15 minutes)
- 0.5 oz (14 g) East Kent Goldings hops (5 minutes)
- English Ale yeast (e.g., Wyeast 1968 or Safale S-04)
- 5 gallons (19 liters) of water (for brewing)
- Priming sugar (for bottling)

Instructions:

1. Mashing:

- Heat 3.5 gallons (13 liters) of water to around 165°F (74°C).
- Add crushed grains to a grain bag and steep in the water for 60 minutes at a temperature around 152°F (67°C).
- Remove the grain bag and let it drain into the kettle. Sparge with additional water if necessary.

2. Boiling:

- Bring the wort to a boil and add the pumpkin puree, stirring to incorporate.
- Add 0.5 oz of East Kent Goldings hops and boil for 45 minutes.
- Add Pumpkin Pie Spice and Whirlfloc tablet at 15 minutes.
- Add the remaining 0.5 oz of East Kent Goldings hops at 5 minutes.

3. Cooling and Fermentation:

- Cool the wort quickly using a wort chiller or an ice bath to around 68°F (20°C).
- Transfer the cooled wort to a sanitized fermenter and top up with water to reach a total volume of 5 gallons (19 liters).
- Aerate the wort and pitch the English Ale yeast.

4. Fermentation:

- Ferment at a temperature of around 65-70°F (18-21°C) for 2-3 weeks or until fermentation is complete.

5. Bottling:

- Once fermentation is complete and the beer has cleared, mix priming sugar into the beer and transfer to sanitized bottles.
- Cap the bottles and allow them to carbonate for at least 2-3 weeks.

6. Conditioning:

- Store the bottled beer in a cool, dark place for a few weeks to allow it to condition and carbonate fully.

7. Enjoy:

- Chill the beer, pour into a pint glass, and savor the delightful blend of pumpkin and spices in your homemade Pumpkin Ale!

Note: Adjust the recipe according to your brewing setup and preferences. Ensure proper sanitation throughout the brewing process for the best results.

Fruit-infused Blonde Ale

Ingredients:

- 8 lbs (3.63 kg) Pale malt
- 1 lb (0.45 kg) Munich malt
- 0.5 lb (0.23 kg) Honey malt
- 1 oz (28 g) Cascade hops (60 minutes)
- 0.5 oz (14 g) Cascade hops (15 minutes)
- 1 Whirlfloc tablet (15 minutes)
- 0.5 oz (14 g) Cascade hops (5 minutes)
- Fruit of your choice (e.g., peaches, apricots, berries) - amount will depend on personal preference and desired fruit intensity
- American Ale yeast (e.g., Wyeast 1056 or Safale US-05)
- 5 gallons (19 liters) of water (for brewing)
- Priming sugar (for bottling)

Instructions:

1. Mashing:

- Heat 3.5 gallons (13 liters) of water to around 165°F (74°C).
- Add crushed grains to a grain bag and steep in the water for 60 minutes at a temperature around 152°F (67°C).
- Remove the grain bag and let it drain into the kettle. Sparge with additional water if necessary.

2. Boiling:

- Bring the wort to a boil and add 1 oz of Cascade hops.
- Boil for 45 minutes, then add 0.5 oz of Cascade hops and the Whirlfloc tablet.
- Continue boiling for an additional 10 minutes, then add the remaining 0.5 oz of Cascade hops.

3. Cooling and Fermentation:

- Cool the wort quickly using a wort chiller or an ice bath to around 68°F (20°C).

- Transfer the cooled wort to a sanitized fermenter and top up with water to reach a total volume of 5 gallons (19 liters).
- Aerate the wort and pitch the American Ale yeast.

4. Primary Fermentation:

- Allow the beer to ferment for about a week in the primary fermenter.

5. Fruit Infusion:

- Prepare the fruit by washing, chopping, and sanitizing.
- Transfer the beer to a secondary fermenter and add the prepared fruit. The amount of fruit will depend on personal preference, but a common range is 1 to 2 lbs of fruit per gallon of beer.
- Seal the fermenter and let it sit for an additional week, allowing the fruit flavors to infuse into the beer.

6. Bottling:

- Once fermentation is complete and the desired fruit intensity is achieved, mix priming sugar into the beer and transfer to sanitized bottles.
- Cap the bottles and allow them to carbonate for at least 2-3 weeks.

7. Conditioning:

- Store the bottled beer in a cool, dark place for a few weeks to allow it to condition and carbonate fully.

8. Enjoy:

- Chill the beer, pour into a glass, and savor the refreshing and fruity notes of your homemade Fruit-Infused Blonde Ale!

Note: Adjust the recipe according to your brewing setup and preferences. Ensure proper sanitation throughout the brewing process for the best results. The choice of fruit can be adjusted based on personal taste and seasonal availability.

Honey Ale

Ingredients:

- 8 lbs (3.63 kg) Pale malt
- 1 lb (0.45 kg) Munich malt
- 0.5 lb (0.23 kg) Honey malt
- 1 lb (0.45 kg) Honey (for late addition)
- 1 oz (28 g) Cascade hops (60 minutes)
- 0.5 oz (14 g) Cascade hops (15 minutes)
- 1 Whirlfloc tablet (15 minutes)
- 0.5 oz (14 g) Cascade hops (5 minutes)
- American Ale yeast (e.g., Wyeast 1056 or Safale US-05)
- 5 gallons (19 liters) of water (for brewing)
- Priming sugar (for bottling)

Instructions:

1. Mashing:

- Heat 3.5 gallons (13 liters) of water to around 165°F (74°C).
- Add crushed grains to a grain bag and steep in the water for 60 minutes at a temperature around 152°F (67°C).
- Remove the grain bag and let it drain into the kettle. Sparge with additional water if necessary.

2. Boiling:

- Bring the wort to a boil and add 1 oz of Cascade hops.
- Boil for 45 minutes, then add 0.5 oz of Cascade hops and the Whirlfloc tablet.
- Continue boiling for an additional 10 minutes, then add the remaining 0.5 oz of Cascade hops.

3. Honey Addition:

- Add 1 lb of honey to the boil during the last 5 minutes.

4. Cooling and Fermentation:

- Cool the wort quickly using a wort chiller or an ice bath to around 68°F (20°C).
- Transfer the cooled wort to a sanitized fermenter and top up with water to reach a total volume of 5 gallons (19 liters).
- Aerate the wort and pitch the American Ale yeast.

5. Fermentation:

- Ferment at a temperature of around 65-70°F (18-21°C) for 2-3 weeks or until fermentation is complete.

6. Bottling:

- Once fermentation is complete, mix priming sugar into the beer and transfer to sanitized bottles.
- Cap the bottles and allow them to carbonate for at least 2-3 weeks.

7. Conditioning:

- Store the bottled beer in a cool, dark place for a few weeks to allow it to condition and carbonate fully.

8. Enjoy:

- Chill the beer, pour into a glass, and appreciate the smooth sweetness and subtle honey notes of your homemade Honey Ale!

Note: Adjust the recipe according to your brewing setup and preferences. Ensure proper sanitation throughout the brewing process for the best results.

Coffee Stout

Ingredients:

- 8 lbs (3.63 kg) Maris Otter malt
- 1 lb (0.45 kg) Flaked barley
- 1 lb (0.45 kg) Chocolate malt
- 0.5 lb (0.23 kg) Black Patent malt
- 1 lb (0.45 kg) Caramel/Crystal malt (60L)
- 1 oz (28 g) East Kent Goldings hops (60 minutes)
- 1 Whirlfloc tablet (15 minutes)
- 1 lb (0.45 kg) lactose (optional, for sweetness and body)
- 8 oz (227 g) coarsely ground coffee (cold brewed) - for post-fermentation addition
- English Ale yeast (e.g., Wyeast 1968 or Safale S-04)
- 5 gallons (19 liters) of water (for brewing)
- Priming sugar (for bottling)

Instructions:

1. Mashing:

- Heat 3.5 gallons (13 liters) of water to around 165°F (74°C).
- Add crushed grains to a grain bag and steep in the water for 60 minutes at a temperature around 152°F (67°C).
- Remove the grain bag and let it drain into the kettle. Sparge with additional water if necessary.

2. Boiling:

- Bring the wort to a boil and add 1 oz of East Kent Goldings hops.
- Boil for 45 minutes, then add the Whirlfloc tablet.
- Continue boiling for an additional 15 minutes.

3. Cooling and Fermentation:

- Cool the wort quickly using a wort chiller or an ice bath to around 68°F (20°C).
- Transfer the cooled wort to a sanitized fermenter and top up with water to reach a total volume of 5 gallons (19 liters).
- Aerate the wort and pitch the English Ale yeast.

4. Fermentation:

- Ferment at a temperature of around 65-70°F (18-21°C) for 2-3 weeks or until fermentation is complete.

5. Cold Brew Coffee Addition:

- Prepare cold brew coffee by coarsely grinding coffee beans and steeping them in cold water for 12-24 hours.
- After primary fermentation is complete, add the cold brew coffee to the fermenter. Start with a small amount and taste, adding more if needed to achieve the desired coffee flavor.

6. Bottling:

- Once fermentation is complete and the desired coffee flavor is achieved, mix priming sugar into the beer and transfer to sanitized bottles.
- Cap the bottles and allow them to carbonate for at least 2-3 weeks.

7. Conditioning:

- Store the bottled beer in a cool, dark place for several weeks to allow it to condition and carbonate fully.

8. Enjoy:

- Chill the beer, pour into a stout glass, and savor the rich and bold combination of your homemade Coffee Stout!

Note: Adjust the recipe according to your brewing setup and preferences. Ensure proper sanitation throughout the brewing process for the best results. Experiment with the amount of coffee to achieve the desired level of coffee flavor.

Chocolate Cherry Porter

Ingredients:

- 7 lbs (3.18 kg) Maris Otter malt
- 1 lb (0.45 kg) Chocolate malt
- 0.5 lb (0.23 kg) Munich malt
- 0.5 lb (0.23 kg) Caramel/Crystal malt (60L)
- 0.5 lb (0.23 kg) Black Patent malt
- 1 lb (0.45 kg) Flaked barley
- 1 oz (28 g) East Kent Goldings hops (60 minutes)
- 1 Whirlfloc tablet (15 minutes)
- 4 oz (113 g) Cocoa nibs (in secondary fermentation)
- 1 lb (0.45 kg) Cherries (frozen, pitted, and thawed) - for secondary fermentation
- English Ale yeast (e.g., Wyeast 1968 or Safale S-04)
- 5 gallons (19 liters) of water (for brewing)
- Priming sugar (for bottling)

Instructions:

1. Mashing:

- Heat 3.5 gallons (13 liters) of water to around 165°F (74°C).
- Add crushed grains to a grain bag and steep in the water for 60 minutes at a temperature around 152°F (67°C).
- Remove the grain bag and let it drain into the kettle. Sparge with additional water if necessary.

2. Boiling:

- Bring the wort to a boil and add 1 oz of East Kent Goldings hops.
- Boil for 45 minutes, then add the Whirlfloc tablet.
- Continue boiling for an additional 15 minutes.

3. Cooling and Fermentation:

- Cool the wort quickly using a wort chiller or an ice bath to around 68°F (20°C).
- Transfer the cooled wort to a sanitized fermenter and top up with water to reach a total volume of 5 gallons (19 liters).
- Aerate the wort and pitch the English Ale yeast.

4. Primary Fermentation:

- Ferment at a temperature of around 65-70°F (18-21°C) for 1-2 weeks or until fermentation is complete.

5. Secondary Fermentation:

- Transfer the beer to a secondary fermenter.
- Add cocoa nibs and thawed cherries to the secondary fermenter. Consider placing the cherries in a sanitized mesh bag for easier removal later.
- Allow the beer to ferment for an additional 2-3 weeks.

6. Bottling:

- Once fermentation is complete and the desired flavors are achieved, remove the cocoa nibs and cherries, and mix priming sugar into the beer.
- Transfer the beer to sanitized bottles.
- Cap the bottles and allow them to carbonate for at least 2-3 weeks.

7. Conditioning:

- Store the bottled beer in a cool, dark place for several weeks to allow it to condition and carbonate fully.

8. Enjoy:

- Chill the beer, pour into a porter glass, and savor the delightful combination of chocolate and cherry in your homemade Chocolate Cherry Porter!

Note: Adjust the recipe according to your brewing setup and preferences. Ensure proper sanitation throughout the brewing process for the best results. Experiment with the amount of cocoa nibs and cherries to achieve the desired flavor balance.

Gingerbread Spiced Ale

Ingredients:

- 8 lbs (3.63 kg) Maris Otter malt
- 1 lb (0.45 kg) Munich malt
- 0.5 lb (0.23 kg) Caramel/Crystal malt (60L)
- 0.5 lb (0.23 kg) Caramel/Crystal malt (120L)
- 1 lb (0.45 kg) Flaked oats
- 1 oz (28 g) East Kent Goldings hops (60 minutes)
- 1 Whirlfloc tablet (15 minutes)
- 1 tsp Ground ginger (15 minutes)
- 1 tsp Ground cinnamon (15 minutes)
- 0.5 tsp Ground nutmeg (15 minutes)
- 0.25 tsp Ground cloves (15 minutes)
- 0.25 tsp Allspice (15 minutes)
- 1 oz (28 g) East Kent Goldings hops (5 minutes)
- English Ale yeast (e.g., Wyeast 1968 or Safale S-04)
- 5 gallons (19 liters) of water (for brewing)
- Priming sugar (for bottling)

Instructions:

1. Mashing:

- Heat 3.5 gallons (13 liters) of water to around 165°F (74°C).
- Add crushed grains to a grain bag and steep in the water for 60 minutes at a temperature around 152°F (67°C).
- Remove the grain bag and let it drain into the kettle. Sparge with additional water if necessary.

2. Boiling:

- Bring the wort to a boil and add 1 oz of East Kent Goldings hops.
- Boil for 45 minutes, then add the Whirlfloc tablet, ground ginger, ground cinnamon, ground nutmeg, ground cloves, and allspice.
- Continue boiling for an additional 10 minutes, then add the remaining 1 oz of East Kent Goldings hops.

3. Cooling and Fermentation:

- Cool the wort quickly using a wort chiller or an ice bath to around 68°F (20°C).
- Transfer the cooled wort to a sanitized fermenter and top up with water to reach a total volume of 5 gallons (19 liters).
- Aerate the wort and pitch the English Ale yeast.

4. Fermentation:

- Ferment at a temperature of around 65-70°F (18-21°C) for 2-3 weeks or until fermentation is complete.

5. Bottling:

- Once fermentation is complete, mix priming sugar into the beer and transfer to sanitized bottles.
- Cap the bottles and allow them to carbonate for at least 2-3 weeks.

6. Conditioning:

- Store the bottled beer in a cool, dark place for a few weeks to allow it to condition and carbonate fully.

7. Enjoy:

- Chill the beer, pour into a festive glass, and savor the warm and spicy notes of your homemade Gingerbread Spiced Ale!

Note: Adjust the recipe according to your brewing setup and preferences. Ensure proper sanitation throughout the brewing process for the best results. You can also experiment with the spice quantities to achieve your desired level of spiciness.

Citrus IPA

Ingredients:

- 8 lbs (3.63 kg) Pale malt
- 1 lb (0.45 kg) Munich malt
- 0.5 lb (0.23 kg) Caramel/Crystal malt (20L)
- 0.5 lb (0.23 kg) Carapils malt
- 1 oz (28 g) Cascade hops (60 minutes)
- 1 oz (28 g) Centennial hops (15 minutes)
- 1 Whirlfloc tablet (15 minutes)
- 1 oz (28 g) Cascade hops (5 minutes)
- Zest of 2 oranges (5 minutes)
- 0.5 oz (14 g) Cascade hops (0 minutes - flameout)
- 1 oz (28 g) Centennial hops (dry hop - after fermentation)
- 1 oz (28 g) Citra hops (dry hop - after fermentation)
- American Ale yeast (e.g., Wyeast 1056 or Safale US-05)
- 5 gallons (19 liters) of water (for brewing)
- Priming sugar (for bottling)

Instructions:

1. Mashing:

- Heat 3.5 gallons (13 liters) of water to around 165°F (74°C).
- Add crushed grains to a grain bag and steep in the water for 60 minutes at a temperature around 152°F (67°C).
- Remove the grain bag and let it drain into the kettle. Sparge with additional water if necessary.

2. Boiling:

- Bring the wort to a boil and add 1 oz of Cascade hops.
- Boil for 45 minutes, then add the Whirlfloc tablet.
- Add Centennial hops, Cascade hops, and orange zest at the specified times during the last 15 minutes of the boil.

3. Cooling and Fermentation:

- Cool the wort quickly using a wort chiller or an ice bath to around 68°F (20°C).

- Transfer the cooled wort to a sanitized fermenter and top up with water to reach a total volume of 5 gallons (19 liters).
- Aerate the wort and pitch the American Ale yeast.

4. Fermentation:

- Ferment at a temperature of around 65-70°F (18-21°C) for 2 weeks.

5. Dry Hopping:

- After primary fermentation, add the Centennial and Citra hops to the fermenter for dry hopping.
- Allow the beer to dry hop for 5-7 days, enhancing the citrus aroma.

6. Bottling:

- Once dry hopping is complete, mix priming sugar into the beer and transfer to sanitized bottles.
- Cap the bottles and allow them to carbonate for at least 2-3 weeks.

7. Conditioning:

- Store the bottled beer in a cool, dark place for a few weeks to allow it to condition and carbonate fully.

8. Enjoy:

- Chill the beer, pour into a pint glass, and revel in the refreshing citrus notes of your homemade Citrus IPA!

Note: Adjust the recipe according to your brewing setup and preferences. Ensure proper sanitation throughout the brewing process for the best results. Feel free to experiment with different citrus varieties or adjust the dry hop amounts for a more pronounced aroma.

Rye Pale Ale

Ingredients:

- 8 lbs (3.63 kg) Pale malt
- 2 lbs (0.91 kg) Rye malt
- 0.5 lb (0.23 kg) Caramel/Crystal malt (40L)
- 0.5 lb (0.23 kg) Carapils malt
- 1 oz (28 g) Cascade hops (60 minutes)
- 1 oz (28 g) Centennial hops (15 minutes)
- 1 Whirlfloc tablet (15 minutes)
- 1 oz (28 g) Cascade hops (5 minutes)
- 1 oz (28 g) Centennial hops (0 minutes - flameout)
- 1 oz (28 g) Cascade hops (dry hop - after fermentation)
- 1 oz (28 g) Centennial hops (dry hop - after fermentation)
- American Ale yeast (e.g., Wyeast 1056 or Safale US-05)
- 5 gallons (19 liters) of water (for brewing)
- Priming sugar (for bottling)

Instructions:

1. Mashing:

- Heat 3.5 gallons (13 liters) of water to around 165°F (74°C).
- Add crushed grains to a grain bag and steep in the water for 60 minutes at a temperature around 152°F (67°C).
- Remove the grain bag and let it drain into the kettle. Sparge with additional water if necessary.

2. Boiling:

- Bring the wort to a boil and add 1 oz of Cascade hops.
- Boil for 45 minutes, then add the Whirlfloc tablet.
- Add Centennial hops and Cascade hops at the specified times during the last 15 minutes of the boil.

3. Cooling and Fermentation:

- Cool the wort quickly using a wort chiller or an ice bath to around 68°F (20°C).
- Transfer the cooled wort to a sanitized fermenter and top up with water to reach a total volume of 5 gallons (19 liters).
- Aerate the wort and pitch the American Ale yeast.

4. Fermentation:

- Ferment at a temperature of around 65-70°F (18-21°C) for 2 weeks.

5. Dry Hopping:

- After primary fermentation, add the Cascade and Centennial hops to the fermenter for dry hopping.
- Allow the beer to dry hop for 5-7 days, enhancing the hop aroma.

6. Bottling:

- Once dry hopping is complete, mix priming sugar into the beer and transfer to sanitized bottles.
- Cap the bottles and allow them to carbonate for at least 2-3 weeks.

7. Conditioning:

- Store the bottled beer in a cool, dark place for a few weeks to allow it to condition and carbonate fully.

8. Enjoy:

- Chill the beer, pour into a pint glass, and savor the unique character of your homemade Rye Pale Ale!

Note: Adjust the recipe according to your brewing setup and preferences. Ensure proper sanitation throughout the brewing process for the best results. The addition of rye malt will contribute to a distinctive spiciness and mouthfeel in the finished beer.

Smoked Porter

Ingredients:

- 8 lbs (3.63 kg) Maris Otter malt
- 1 lb (0.45 kg) Smoked malt (Beechwood or Cherrywood smoked malt)
- 0.5 lb (0.23 kg) Chocolate malt
- 0.5 lb (0.23 kg) Munich malt
- 0.5 lb (0.23 kg) Caramel/Crystal malt (60L)
- 0.25 lb (0.11 kg) Black Patent malt
- 1 oz (28 g) East Kent Goldings hops (60 minutes)
- 0.5 oz (14 g) East Kent Goldings hops (15 minutes)
- 1 Whirlfloc tablet (15 minutes)
- 0.5 oz (14 g) East Kent Goldings hops (5 minutes)
- English Ale yeast (e.g., Wyeast 1968 or Safale S-04)
- 5 gallons (19 liters) of water (for brewing)
- Priming sugar (for bottling)

Instructions:

1. Mashing:

- Heat 3.5 gallons (13 liters) of water to around 165°F (74°C).
- Add crushed grains to a grain bag and steep in the water for 60 minutes at a temperature around 152°F (67°C).
- Remove the grain bag and let it drain into the kettle. Sparge with additional water if necessary.

2. Boiling:

- Bring the wort to a boil and add 1 oz of East Kent Goldings hops.
- Boil for 45 minutes, then add the Whirlfloc tablet.
- Add 0.5 oz of East Kent Goldings hops at 15 minutes and the remaining 0.5 oz at 5 minutes.

3. Cooling and Fermentation:

- Cool the wort quickly using a wort chiller or an ice bath to around 68°F (20°C).
- Transfer the cooled wort to a sanitized fermenter and top up with water to reach a total volume of 5 gallons (19 liters).

- Aerate the wort and pitch the English Ale yeast.

4. Fermentation:

- Ferment at a temperature of around 65-70°F (18-21°C) for 2-3 weeks or until fermentation is complete.

5. Bottling:

- Once fermentation is complete, mix priming sugar into the beer and transfer to sanitized bottles.
- Cap the bottles and allow them to carbonate for at least 2-3 weeks.

6. Conditioning:

- Store the bottled beer in a cool, dark place for several weeks to allow it to condition and carbonate fully.

7. Enjoy:

- Chill the beer, pour into a pint glass, and savor the rich and smoky notes of your homemade Smoked Porter!

Note: Adjust the recipe according to your brewing setup and preferences. Ensure proper sanitation throughout the brewing process for the best results. The choice of smoked malt can influence the intensity and character of the smokiness, so you may adjust the quantity based on your preference.

Saison

Ingredients:

- 9 lbs (4.08 kg) Pilsner malt
- 1 lb (0.45 kg) Munich malt
- 1 lb (0.45 kg) Wheat malt
- 0.5 lb (0.23 kg) Vienna malt
- 0.5 lb (0.23 kg) Cane sugar (added late in the boil)
- 1 oz (28 g) Saaz hops (60 minutes)
- 0.5 oz (14 g) Saaz hops (15 minutes)
- 1 Whirlfloc tablet (15 minutes)
- 0.5 oz (14 g) Saaz hops (5 minutes)
- Belgian Saison yeast (e.g., Wyeast 3711 or Belle Saison)
- 5 gallons (19 liters) of water (for brewing)
- Priming sugar (for bottling)

Instructions:

1. Mashing:

- Heat 3.5 gallons (13 liters) of water to around 165°F (74°C).
- Add crushed grains to a grain bag and steep in the water for 60 minutes at a temperature around 145-155°F (63-68°C).
- Remove the grain bag and let it drain into the kettle. Sparge with additional water if necessary.

2. Boiling:

- Bring the wort to a boil and add 1 oz of Saaz hops.
- Boil for 45 minutes, then add the Whirlfloc tablet.
- Add 0.5 oz of Saaz hops at 15 minutes and the remaining 0.5 oz at 5 minutes.
- Add the cane sugar late in the boil (last 10 minutes).

3. Cooling and Fermentation:

- Cool the wort quickly using a wort chiller or an ice bath to around 70-75°F (21-24°C).
- Transfer the cooled wort to a sanitized fermenter and top up with water to reach a total volume of 5 gallons (19 liters).
- Aerate the wort and pitch the Belgian Saison yeast.

4. Fermentation:

- Ferment at a temperature of around 70-75°F (21-24°C) for the first few days, then you can allow the temperature to rise to encourage yeast character. Saison yeast strains can tolerate higher fermentation temperatures.

5. Bottling:

- Once fermentation is complete, mix priming sugar into the beer and transfer to sanitized bottles.
- Cap the bottles and allow them to carbonate for at least 2-3 weeks.

6. Conditioning:

- Store the bottled beer in a cool, dark place for several weeks to allow it to condition and carbonate fully.

7. Enjoy:

- Chill the beer, pour into a tulip glass, and enjoy the fruity and spicy flavors with the characteristic dry finish of your homemade Saison!

Note: Adjust the recipe according to your brewing setup and preferences. Saison yeast strains can produce a range of flavors, and fermentation temperature control can influence the final profile. Feel free to experiment with different Saison yeast strains for unique variations.

Mocha Milk Stout

Ingredients:

- 8 lbs (3.63 kg) Maris Otter malt
- 1 lb (0.45 kg) Chocolate malt
- 1 lb (0.45 kg) Munich malt
- 0.5 lb (0.23 kg) Caramel/Crystal malt (60L)
- 0.5 lb (0.23 kg) Flaked oats
- 1 lb (0.45 kg) Lactose (added at the end of the boil)
- 1 oz (28 g) East Kent Goldings hops (60 minutes)
- 1 Whirlfloc tablet (15 minutes)
- 4 oz (113 g) Cocoa nibs (in secondary fermentation)
- 4 oz (113 g) Coarsely ground coffee (cold brewed) - for post-fermentation addition
- English Ale yeast (e.g., Wyeast 1968 or Safale S-04)
- 5 gallons (19 liters) of water (for brewing)
- Priming sugar (for bottling)

Instructions:

1. Mashing:

- Heat 3.5 gallons (13 liters) of water to around 165°F (74°C).
- Add crushed grains to a grain bag and steep in the water for 60 minutes at a temperature around 152°F (67°C).
- Remove the grain bag and let it drain into the kettle. Sparge with additional water if necessary.

2. Boiling:

- Bring the wort to a boil and add 1 oz of East Kent Goldings hops.
- Boil for 45 minutes, then add the Whirlfloc tablet.
- Add lactose to the boil during the last 15 minutes.

3. Cooling and Fermentation:

- Cool the wort quickly using a wort chiller or an ice bath to around 68°F (20°C).
- Transfer the cooled wort to a sanitized fermenter and top up with water to reach a total volume of 5 gallons (19 liters).
- Aerate the wort and pitch the English Ale yeast.

4. Primary Fermentation:

- Ferment at a temperature of around 65-70°F (18-21°C) for 1-2 weeks or until fermentation is complete.

5. Secondary Fermentation:

- Transfer the beer to a secondary fermenter.
- Add cocoa nibs to the secondary fermenter, ensuring they are sanitized. Allow the beer to ferment for an additional 1-2 weeks.

6. Cold Brew Coffee Addition:

- Prepare cold brew coffee by coarsely grinding coffee beans and steeping them in cold water for 12-24 hours.
- After primary and secondary fermentation is complete, add the cold brew coffee to the fermenter. Start with a small amount and taste, adding more if needed to achieve the desired coffee flavor.

7. Bottling:

- Once fermentation and flavor development are complete, mix priming sugar into the beer and transfer to sanitized bottles.
- Cap the bottles and allow them to carbonate for at least 2-3 weeks.

8. Conditioning:

- Store the bottled beer in a cool, dark place for several weeks to allow it to condition and carbonate fully.

9. Enjoy:

- Chill the beer, pour into a stout glass, and savor the delightful combination of chocolate, coffee, and lactose sweetness in your homemade Mocha Milk Stout!

Note: Adjust the recipe according to your brewing setup and preferences. Ensure proper sanitation throughout the brewing process for the best results. Experiment with the amount of cocoa nibs and cold brew coffee to achieve the desired flavor balance.

Coconut Cream Ale

Ingredients:

- 8 lbs (3.63 kg) Pale malt
- 1 lb (0.45 kg) Flaked corn
- 0.5 lb (0.23 kg) Munich malt
- 0.5 lb (0.23 kg) Carapils malt
- 1 oz (28 g) Saaz hops (60 minutes)
- 1 Whirlfloc tablet (15 minutes)
- 0.5 oz (14 g) Saaz hops (5 minutes)
- 1 lb (0.45 kg) Sweetened shredded coconut (toasted) - added after primary fermentation
- American Ale yeast (e.g., Wyeast 1056 or Safale US-05)
- 5 gallons (19 liters) of water (for brewing)
- Priming sugar (for bottling)

Instructions:

1. Mashing:

- Heat 3.5 gallons (13 liters) of water to around 165°F (74°C).
- Add crushed grains to a grain bag and steep in the water for 60 minutes at a temperature around 150°F (65°C).
- Remove the grain bag and let it drain into the kettle. Sparge with additional water if necessary.

2. Boiling:

- Bring the wort to a boil and add 1 oz of Saaz hops.
- Boil for 45 minutes, then add the Whirlfloc tablet.
- Add 0.5 oz of Saaz hops at 5 minutes.

3. Cooling and Fermentation:

- Cool the wort quickly using a wort chiller or an ice bath to around 68°F (20°C).
- Transfer the cooled wort to a sanitized fermenter and top up with water to reach a total volume of 5 gallons (19 liters).
- Aerate the wort and pitch the American Ale yeast.

4. Primary Fermentation:

- Ferment at a temperature of around 65-70°F (18-21°C) for 1-2 weeks or until fermentation is complete.

5. Toasted Coconut Addition:

- Toast the shredded coconut in an oven until golden brown. Be careful not to burn it.
- Add the toasted coconut to the fermenter after primary fermentation is complete.

6. Secondary Fermentation:

- Allow the beer to ferment with the added coconut for an additional 1-2 weeks.

7. Bottling:

- Once fermentation is complete and the desired coconut flavor is achieved, mix priming sugar into the beer and transfer to sanitized bottles.
- Cap the bottles and allow them to carbonate for at least 2-3 weeks.

8. Conditioning:

- Store the bottled beer in a cool, dark place for several weeks to allow it to condition and carbonate fully.

9. Enjoy:

- Chill the beer, pour into a pint glass, and relish the tropical and creamy notes of your homemade Coconut Cream Ale!

Note: Adjust the recipe according to your brewing setup and preferences. Ensure proper sanitation throughout the brewing process for the best results. Experiment with the amount of toasted coconut to achieve the desired coconut flavor.

Black IPA

Ingredients:

- 8 lbs (3.63 kg) Pale malt
- 1 lb (0.45 kg) Munich malt
- 1 lb (0.45 kg) Carafa III malt (or other de-husked black malt)
- 0.5 lb (0.23 kg) Caramel/Crystal malt (60L)
- 0.5 lb (0.23 kg) Victory malt
- 0.5 lb (0.23 kg) Carapils malt
- 1 oz (28 g) Columbus hops (60 minutes)
- 1 oz (28 g) Centennial hops (15 minutes)
- 1 Whirlfloc tablet (15 minutes)
- 1 oz (28 g) Centennial hops (5 minutes)
- 1 oz (28 g) Cascade hops (0 minutes - flameout)
- 1 oz (28 g) Centennial hops (dry hop - after fermentation)
- 1 oz (28 g) Cascade hops (dry hop - after fermentation)
- American Ale yeast (e.g., Wyeast 1056 or Safale US-05)
- 5 gallons (19 liters) of water (for brewing)
- Priming sugar (for bottling)

Instructions:

1. Mashing:

- Heat 3.5 gallons (13 liters) of water to around 165°F (74°C).
- Add crushed grains to a grain bag and steep in the water for 60 minutes at a temperature around 150°F (65°C).
- Remove the grain bag and let it drain into the kettle. Sparge with additional water if necessary.

2. Boiling:

- Bring the wort to a boil and add 1 oz of Columbus hops.
- Boil for 45 minutes, then add the Whirlfloc tablet.
- Add Centennial hops at 15 minutes, and Cascade hops at 5 minutes. Add the remaining Cascade hops at flameout.

3. Cooling and Fermentation:

- Cool the wort quickly using a wort chiller or an ice bath to around 68°F (20°C).
- Transfer the cooled wort to a sanitized fermenter and top up with water to reach a total volume of 5 gallons (19 liters).
- Aerate the wort and pitch the American Ale yeast.

4. Fermentation:

- Ferment at a temperature of around 65-70°F (18-21°C) for 2 weeks.

5. Dry Hopping:

- After primary fermentation, add the Centennial and Cascade hops to the fermenter for dry hopping.
- Allow the beer to dry hop for 5-7 days, enhancing the hop aroma.

6. Bottling:

- Once dry hopping is complete, mix priming sugar into the beer and transfer to sanitized bottles.
- Cap the bottles and allow them to carbonate for at least 2-3 weeks.

7. Conditioning:

- Store the bottled beer in a cool, dark place for several weeks to allow it to condition and carbonate fully.

8. Enjoy:

- Chill the beer, pour into a pint glass, and relish the bold and contrasting flavors of your homemade Black IPA!

Note: Adjust the recipe according to your brewing setup and preferences. Ensure proper sanitation throughout the brewing process for the best results. Experiment with different hop varieties or adjust the malt bill to suit your taste preferences.

Raspberry Wheat Beer

Ingredients:

- 5 lbs (2.27 kg) Wheat malt
- 4 lbs (1.81 kg) Pale malt
- 1 lb (0.45 kg) Flaked wheat
- 1 oz (28 g) Saaz hops (60 minutes)
- 1 Whirlfloc tablet (15 minutes)
- 1 oz (28 g) Saaz hops (5 minutes)
- 3 lbs (1.36 kg) Raspberries (fresh or frozen) - added after primary fermentation
- American Wheat yeast (e.g., Wyeast 1010 or Safale US-05)
- 5 gallons (19 liters) of water (for brewing)
- Priming sugar (for bottling)

Instructions:

1. Mashing:

- Heat 3.5 gallons (13 liters) of water to around 165°F (74°C).
- Add crushed grains to a grain bag and steep in the water for 60 minutes at a temperature around 152°F (67°C).
- Remove the grain bag and let it drain into the kettle. Sparge with additional water if necessary.

2. Boiling:

- Bring the wort to a boil and add 1 oz of Saaz hops.
- Boil for 45 minutes, then add the Whirlfloc tablet.
- Add 1 oz of Saaz hops at 5 minutes.

3. Cooling and Fermentation:

- Cool the wort quickly using a wort chiller or an ice bath to around 68°F (20°C).
- Transfer the cooled wort to a sanitized fermenter and top up with water to reach a total volume of 5 gallons (19 liters).
- Aerate the wort and pitch the American Wheat yeast.

4. Primary Fermentation:

- Ferment at a temperature of around 65-70°F (18-21°C) for 1-2 weeks.

5. Raspberry Addition:

    - After primary fermentation is complete, add the raspberries to the fermenter.
    - You can either crush the raspberries or freeze them beforehand to help break down cell walls and release more flavor.
    - Allow the beer to ferment with the raspberries for an additional 1-2 weeks.

6. Bottling:

    - Once fermentation is complete and the desired raspberry flavor is achieved, mix priming sugar into the beer and transfer to sanitized bottles.
    - Cap the bottles and allow them to carbonate for at least 2-3 weeks.

7. Conditioning:

    - Store the bottled beer in a cool, dark place for several weeks to allow it to condition and carbonate fully.

8. Enjoy:

    - Chill the beer, pour into a wheat beer glass, and savor the refreshing and fruity notes of your homemade Raspberry Wheat Beer!

Note: Adjust the recipe according to your brewing setup and preferences. Ensure proper sanitation throughout the brewing process for the best results. Experiment with the quantity of raspberries based on your preference for the level of fruitiness.

Oatmeal Stout

Ingredients:

- 7 lbs (3.18 kg) Maris Otter malt
- 1 lb (0.45 kg) Flaked oats
- 1 lb (0.45 kg) Chocolate malt
- 0.75 lb (0.34 kg) Caramel/Crystal malt (60L)
- 0.5 lb (0.23 kg) Munich malt
- 0.25 lb (0.11 kg) Black Patent malt
- 1 oz (28 g) East Kent Goldings hops (60 minutes)
- 1 Whirlfloc tablet (15 minutes)
- 0.5 oz (14 g) East Kent Goldings hops (10 minutes)
- English Ale yeast (e.g., Wyeast 1968 or Safale S-04)
- 5 gallons (19 liters) of water (for brewing)
- Priming sugar (for bottling)

Instructions:

1. Mashing:

- Heat 3.5 gallons (13 liters) of water to around 165°F (74°C).
- Add crushed grains to a grain bag and steep in the water for 60 minutes at a temperature around 155°F (68°C).
- Remove the grain bag and let it drain into the kettle. Sparge with additional water if necessary.

2. Boiling:

- Bring the wort to a boil and add 1 oz of East Kent Goldings hops.
- Boil for 50 minutes, then add the Whirlfloc tablet.
- Add 0.5 oz of East Kent Goldings hops at 10 minutes.

3. Cooling and Fermentation:

- Cool the wort quickly using a wort chiller or an ice bath to around 68°F (20°C).

- Transfer the cooled wort to a sanitized fermenter and top up with water to reach a total volume of 5 gallons (19 liters).
- Aerate the wort and pitch the English Ale yeast.

4. Fermentation:

- Ferment at a temperature of around 65-70°F (18-21°C) for 2-3 weeks or until fermentation is complete.

5. Bottling:

- Once fermentation is complete, mix priming sugar into the beer and transfer to sanitized bottles.
- Cap the bottles and allow them to carbonate for at least 2-3 weeks.

6. Conditioning:

- Store the bottled beer in a cool, dark place for several weeks to allow it to condition and carbonate fully.

7. Enjoy:

- Chill the beer, pour into a stout glass, and appreciate the velvety smoothness and roasted flavors of your homemade Oatmeal Stout!

Note: Adjust the recipe according to your brewing setup and preferences. Ensure proper sanitation throughout the brewing process for the best results. Oats contribute to the beer's creamy mouthfeel, and adjusting their quantity can affect the overall texture of the stout.

Lemon Ginger Shandy

Ingredients:

- 4 lbs (1.81 kg) Pilsner malt
- 1 lb (0.45 kg) Wheat malt
- 0.5 lb (0.23 kg) Flaked wheat
- 0.5 lb (0.23 kg) Munich malt
- 1 oz (28 g) Saaz hops (60 minutes)
- Zest of 3 lemons (5 minutes)
- 1 Whirlfloc tablet (15 minutes)
- 1 lb (0.45 kg) Fresh ginger, peeled and sliced (5 minutes)
- 0.5 oz (14 g) Saaz hops (0 minutes - flameout)
- American Ale yeast (e.g., Wyeast 1056 or Safale US-05)
- 5 gallons (19 liters) of water (for brewing)
- Priming sugar (for bottling)
- Lemonade (to top up, ratio to taste)

Instructions:

1. Mashing:

- Heat 3.5 gallons (13 liters) of water to around 165°F (74°C).
- Add crushed grains to a grain bag and steep in the water for 60 minutes at a temperature around 150°F (65°C).
- Remove the grain bag and let it drain into the kettle. Sparge with additional water if necessary.

2. Boiling:

- Bring the wort to a boil and add 1 oz of Saaz hops.
- Boil for 55 minutes, then add the Whirlfloc tablet.
- Add the lemon zest and fresh ginger at 5 minutes.
- Add 0.5 oz of Saaz hops at flameout.

3. Cooling and Fermentation:

- Cool the wort quickly using a wort chiller or an ice bath to around 68°F (20°C).
- Transfer the cooled wort to a sanitized fermenter and top up with water to reach a total volume of 5 gallons (19 liters).
- Aerate the wort and pitch the American Ale yeast.

4. Fermentation:

- Ferment at a temperature of around 65-70°F (18-21°C) for 2 weeks.

5. Bottling:

- Once fermentation is complete, mix priming sugar into the beer and transfer to sanitized bottles.
- Cap the bottles and allow them to carbonate for at least 2-3 weeks.

6. Shandy Mixing:

- When serving, mix the beer with chilled lemonade to your desired ratio. A common starting point is a 50:50 mix, but you can adjust to taste.

7. Enjoy:

- Chill the Lemon Ginger Shandy, pour into a glass, and relish the bright, citrusy, and ginger notes of your homemade shandy!

Note: Adjust the recipe according to your brewing setup and preferences. Ensure proper sanitation throughout the brewing process for the best results. The lemon zest and fresh ginger add a zesty and spicy kick to the traditional shandy, making it a perfect summer drink.

Altbier

Ingredients:

- Grains:
    - 7 lbs (3.18 kg) Pilsner malt
    - 2 lbs (0.91 kg) Munich malt
    - 0.5 lb (0.23 kg) Caramel/Crystal malt (60L)
    - 0.25 lb (0.11 kg) Melanoidin malt
    - 0.25 lb (0.11 kg) Chocolate malt (for color adjustment)
- Hops:
    - 1 oz (28 g) Perle hops (60 minutes)
    - 0.5 oz (14 g) Tettnang hops (15 minutes)
    - 0.5 oz (14 g) Tettnang hops (5 minutes)
- Yeast:
    - German Ale yeast (e.g., Wyeast 1007 or White Labs WLP036)
- Water:
    - Use soft water or adjust as needed for a balanced profile.
- Miscellaneous:
    - 1 Whirlfloc tablet (15 minutes)
    - Priming sugar (for bottling)

Instructions:

1. Mashing:

- Heat 3.5 gallons (13 liters) of water to around 165°F (74°C).
- Add crushed grains to a grain bag and steep in the water for 60 minutes at a temperature around 152°F (67°C).
- Remove the grain bag and let it drain into the kettle. Sparge with additional water if necessary.

2. Boiling:

- Bring the wort to a boil and add 1 oz of Perle hops.
- Boil for 45 minutes, then add 0.5 oz of Tettnang hops.
- Add 1 Whirlfloc tablet at 15 minutes.

- Add the remaining 0.5 oz of Tettnang hops at 5 minutes.

3. Cooling and Fermentation:

- Cool the wort quickly using a wort chiller or an ice bath to around 68°F (20°C).
- Transfer the cooled wort to a sanitized fermenter and top up with water to reach a total volume of 5 gallons (19 liters).
- Aerate the wort and pitch the German Ale yeast.

4. Fermentation:

- Ferment at a temperature of around 60-68°F (15-20°C) for 2 weeks.

5. Bottling:

- Once fermentation is complete, mix priming sugar into the beer and transfer to sanitized bottles.
- Cap the bottles and allow them to carbonate for at least 2-3 weeks.

6. Conditioning:

- Store the bottled beer in a cool, dark place for several weeks to allow it to condition and carbonate fully.

7. Enjoy:

- Chill the beer, pour into an Altbier glass, and savor the balanced maltiness and clean finish of your homemade Altbier!

Note: Adjust the recipe according to your brewing setup and preferences. Altbier traditionally undergoes a lagering period, so you can cold condition it for a few weeks after fermentation is complete for a smoother flavor profile.

Double IPA

Ingredients:

- Grains:
    - 12 lbs (5.44 kg) Pale malt
    - 1 lb (0.45 kg) Munich malt
    - 1 lb (0.45 kg) Crystal malt (15L)
    - 0.5 lb (0.23 kg) Carapils malt
    - 0.5 lb (0.23 kg) Caramel/Crystal malt (40L)
- Hops:
    - 2 oz (56 g) Columbus hops (60 minutes)
    - 1 oz (28 g) Centennial hops (15 minutes)
    - 1 oz (28 g) Cascade hops (10 minutes)
    - 1 oz (28 g) Centennial hops (5 minutes)
    - 2 oz (56 g) Citra hops (flameout/whirlpool)
    - 2 oz (56 g) Amarillo hops (flameout/whirlpool)
    - 2 oz (56 g) Centennial hops (dry hop - 7 days)
    - 2 oz (56 g) Citra hops (dry hop - 7 days)
    - 1 oz (28 g) Amarillo hops (dry hop - 7 days)
- Yeast:
    - American Ale yeast (e.g., Wyeast 1056 or Safale US-05)
- Water:
    - Adjust water chemistry to achieve a balanced profile.
- Miscellaneous:
    - 1 Whirlfloc tablet (15 minutes)
    - Priming sugar (for bottling)

Instructions:

1. Mashing:

- Heat 3.5 gallons (13 liters) of water to around 165°F (74°C).
- Add crushed grains to a grain bag and steep in the water for 60 minutes at a temperature around 150°F (65°C).
- Remove the grain bag and let it drain into the kettle. Sparge with additional water if necessary.

2. Boiling:

- Bring the wort to a boil and add 2 oz of Columbus hops.
- Boil for 45 minutes, then add 1 oz of Centennial hops.
- Add 1 Whirlfloc tablet at 15 minutes.
- Add Cascade hops at 10 minutes, Centennial hops at 5 minutes, and whirlpool with Citra and Amarillo hops at flameout.

3. Cooling and Fermentation:

- Cool the wort quickly using a wort chiller or an ice bath to around 68°F (20°C).
- Transfer the cooled wort to a sanitized fermenter and top up with water to reach a total volume of 5 gallons (19 liters).
- Aerate the wort and pitch the American Ale yeast.

4. Fermentation:

- Ferment at a temperature of around 65-70°F (18-21°C) for the first few days, then allow the temperature to rise to enhance hop character.

5. Dry Hopping:

- After primary fermentation is complete, add the dry hop additions directly to the fermenter.
- Dry hop for 7 days to maximize hop aroma.

6. Bottling:

- Once dry hopping is complete, mix priming sugar into the beer and transfer to sanitized bottles.
- Cap the bottles and allow them to carbonate for at least 2-3 weeks.

7. Conditioning:

- Store the bottled beer in a cool, dark place for several weeks to allow it to condition and carbonate fully.

8. Enjoy:

- Chill the Double IPA, pour into a tulip glass, and savor the intense hop flavors and aromas of your homemade Double IPA!

Note: Adjust the recipe according to your brewing setup and preferences. Experiment with different hop varieties and quantities for your desired hop profile. Ensure proper sanitation throughout the brewing process for the best results.

Milkshake IPA

Ingredients:

- Grains:
    - 8 lbs (3.63 kg) Pale malt
    - 2 lbs (0.91 kg) Flaked oats
    - 1 lb (0.45 kg) Wheat malt
    - 0.5 lb (0.23 kg) Munich malt
    - 0.5 lb (0.23 kg) Honey malt
    - 0.5 lb (0.23 kg) Carapils malt
- Hops:
    - 1 oz (28 g) Citra hops (60 minutes)
    - 1 oz (28 g) Citra hops (15 minutes)
    - 1 oz (28 g) Mosaic hops (10 minutes)
    - 1 oz (28 g) Mosaic hops (5 minutes)
    - 2 oz (56 g) Citra hops (flameout/whirlpool)
    - 2 oz (56 g) Mosaic hops (flameout/whirlpool)
    - 2 oz (56 g) Citra hops (dry hop - 3 days)
    - 2 oz (56 g) Mosaic hops (dry hop - 3 days)
- Yeast:
    - London Ale III yeast (e.g., Wyeast 1318 or Safale S-04)
- Water:
    - Adjust water chemistry for a softer profile.
- Miscellaneous:
    - 1 lb (0.45 kg) Lactose (added at 15 minutes)
    - 1 Whirlfloc tablet (15 minutes)
    - 1-2 vanilla beans (split and scraped) - added at flameout/whirlpool
    - 2-3 lbs (0.91-1.36 kg) of fruit puree (e.g., mango, peach, or passion fruit) - added at dry hop or during fermentation
    - Priming sugar (for bottling)

Instructions:

1. Mashing:

- Heat 3.5 gallons (13 liters) of water to around 165°F (74°C).
- Add crushed grains to a grain bag and steep in the water for 60 minutes at a temperature around 152°F (67°C).

- Remove the grain bag and let it drain into the kettle. Sparge with additional water if necessary.

2. Boiling:

- Bring the wort to a boil and add 1 oz of Citra hops.
- Boil for 45 minutes, then add 1 oz of Citra hops.
- Add lactose, Whirlfloc tablet, and 1 oz each of Mosaic and Citra hops at 15 minutes.
- Add 1 oz each of Mosaic and Citra hops at 10 minutes.
- Add the remaining Citra and Mosaic hops at flameout/whirlpool along with the scraped vanilla beans.

3. Cooling and Fermentation:

- Cool the wort quickly using a wort chiller or an ice bath to around 68°F (20°C).
- Transfer the cooled wort to a sanitized fermenter and top up with water to reach a total volume of 5 gallons (19 liters).
- Aerate the wort and pitch the London Ale III yeast.

4. Fermentation:

- Ferment at a temperature of around 65-70°F (18-21°C) for 2 weeks.

5. Dry Hopping and Fruit Addition:

- Add the fruit puree and dry hop with Citra and Mosaic hops for 3 days after primary fermentation.

6. Bottling:

- Once dry hopping is complete, mix priming sugar into the beer and transfer to sanitized bottles.
- Cap the bottles and allow them to carbonate for at least 2-3 weeks.

7. Conditioning:

- Store the bottled beer in a cool, dark place for several weeks to allow it to condition and carbonate fully.

8. Enjoy:

- Chill the Milkshake IPA, pour into a tulip glass, and savor the hazy, fruity, and creamy goodness of your homemade Milkshake IPA!

Note: Adjust the recipe according to your brewing setup and preferences. Experiment with different fruit varieties and hop combinations to create unique flavors. Ensure proper sanitation throughout the brewing process for the best results.

www.ingramcontent.com/pod-product-compliance
Lightning Source LLC
LaVergne TN
LVHW081610060526
838201LV00054B/2185